How I Feel

By Margie O'Hern

Scott Foresman
is an imprint of

Glenview, Illinois • Boston, Massachusetts • Chandler, Arizona •
Upper Saddle River, New Jersey

Photographs

Every effort has been made to secure permission and provide appropriate credit for photographic material. The publisher deeply regrets any omission and pledges to correct errors called to its attention in subsequent editions.

Unless otherwise acknowledged, all photographs are the property of Pearson Education, Inc.

Photo locators denoted as follows: Top (T), Center (C), Bottom (B), Left (L), Right (R), Background (Bkgd)

Opener: ©Jupiter Images/BananaStock/Alamy; **1** ©81a/Alamy; **3** ©Christina Kennedy/Alamy; **4** ©81a/Alamy; **5** Getty Images; **6** ©Jose Luis Pelaez Inc/Photolibrary; **7** ©Blend Images/Getty Images; **8** ©Jupiter Images/BananaStock/Alamy.

ISBN: 13: 978-0-328-46342-8
ISBN 10:   0-328-46342-6

4 5 6 7 8 9 10 V010 14 13 12 11

I love my grandma.

I write a letter about us.

I love my daddy.

I draw a picture of us.

I love my mommy.
I sing a song about us.

I love my brother.

I paint a picture of us.

I love my grandpa.

I write a poem about us.

I love my family.
I take a photo of us.